Soccer

Written by Laurie Wark

Illustrated by Scot Ritchie

Kids Can Press

With much appreciation and many thanks to
Duncan Wilde, Director, Premier Soccer Academy,
for his professional advice and for sharing his
knowledge of the sport and his experience in
teaching the game to children.

Text copyright © 1994 by Laurie Wark
Illustrations copyright © 1994 by Scot Ritchie

Published in Canada by:
Kids Can Press Ltd.
29 Birch Avenue
Toronto, ON M4V 1E2

Published in the U.S. by:
Kids Can Press Ltd.
85 River Rock Drive, Suite 202
Buffalo, NY 14207

Kids Can Press is a Nelvana company

Edited by Debbie Rogosin
Designed by Rob McPhail
Typeset by McPhail & Hemsworth Associates
Printed in Hong Kong by Sheck Wah Tong Printing Press
Limited

CM 94 0 9 8 7 6 5 4 3 2

Canadian Cataloguing in Publication Data

Wark, Laurie
    Soccer

(Basics for beginners)
ISBN 1-55074-188-8

1. Soccer – Juvenile literature. 2. Soccer – Rules – Juvenile
literature. I. Ritchie, Scot. II. Title. III. Series.

GV943.25.W37 1994   j796.334   C94-930249-

People all around the world play soccer. In some
countries the game is called football. Whatever you
call it, soccer is an exciting and fast-moving sport.
Players run back and forth across the field kicking
and passing the ball to each other and trying to shoot
it into the other team's goal. Anyone can play — if
you like to run and you like being part of a team,
you'll have a ball playing soccer.

You don't need much equipment to play soccer. Grab a ball, strap on a pair of shin guards and some soccer shoes, and you're ready to play. Soccer shoes have small spikes, called cleats, on the bottom to help players run, start, stop and change direction quickly. When you play in a league you wear a uniform so that it's easy to tell your team from the other team.

Soccer players must keep fit because they do a lot of running during a game. It's important for everyone on the team to stretch and warm up before each game or practice. Your coach will show you how to stretch your muscles. Then you'll do some practice drills with your teammates to work on important soccer skills like kicking, passing and controlling the ball.

Good work! Move towards the ball to receive
If you stretch for a pass, the ball may bound
off your foot and away from you.

You'll have to learn some fancy footwork to
play soccer — unless the ball goes out of play,
you can't touch it with your hands or arms.
At first you may notice that one leg seems
stronger than the other and that it's easier to
kick the ball with that leg. Practise using each
of your feet to kick the ball so that you'll be
ready to go in any direction.

You'll do a lot of passing during a game to keep the other team from getting the ball. For control and accuracy in passing the ball over short distances, use the inside of your shoe — the part that covers the arch of your foot. You can use the same part of your foot to control the ball when you're receiving passes. Always be on the lookout for a teammate you can pass the ball to.

Now it's time to put the kicking together with running! This is called dribbling. Kick the ball ahead of you from one foot to the other as you run — it will take practice so you don't trip over the ball. Once you can dribble well, try changing your speed or direction to lose opponents who may be trying to get the ball from you.

To get the most power from your kick, use the top of your foot — the part your shoelaces cover.

To score, you must get the ball into the other team's goal. The team with the most goals at the end of the game wins. Practise shooting the ball into the corners of the goal to keep it away from the goalkeeper. For accuracy, always follow through with your kicks. This means that your foot follows the direction of the ball after you've kicked it.

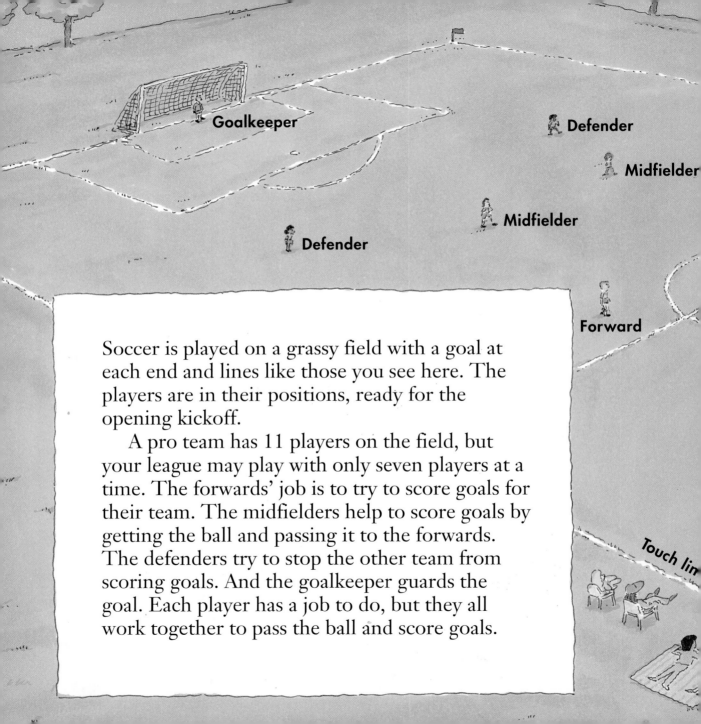

Goalkeeper

Defender

Midfielder

Midfielder

Defender

Forward

Touch lin

Soccer is played on a grassy field with a goal at each end and lines like those you see here. The players are in their positions, ready for the opening kickoff.

A pro team has 11 players on the field, but your league may play with only seven players at a time. The forwards' job is to try to score goals for their team. The midfielders help to score goals by getting the ball and passing it to the forwards. The defenders try to stop the other team from scoring goals. And the goalkeeper guards the goal. Each player has a job to do, but they all work together to pass the ball and score goals.

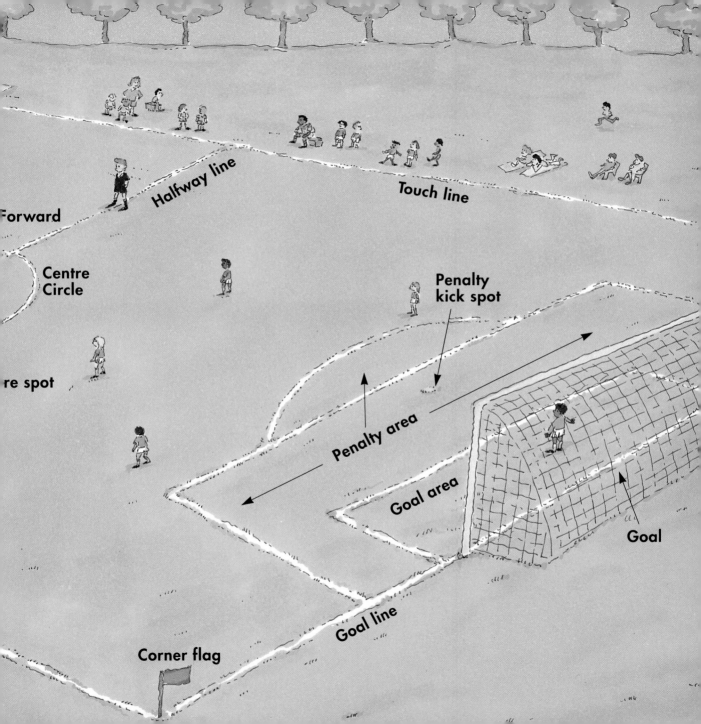

Halfway line

Touch line

Forward

Centre Circle

Penalty kick spot

re spot

Penalty area

Goal area

Goal

Goal line

Corner flag

The Tigers win the coin toss to kick off the game, and the players run down the field, passing the ball from teammate to teammate. Not all the players go after the ball at once: for the best teamwork each player tries to play his or her own position. Soccer is an action-packed game from start to finish. Players on the field change places with their teammates on the sidelines so that everyone gets a chance to play and to rest.

At the end of the first half, the players take a break to rest and have a drink. Then it's back to the field, and the teams change ends to begin the second half.

Andrew heads the ball to Paul, who kicks it over the touch line by accident. A player from the other team throws the ball back in to start play again. For a throw-in, keep your feet on the ground and throw the ball from behind your head with both hands. Try to throw it to a teammate who is not near a player from the other team.

Jason intercepts the ball and passes it to
Yvette. She kicks it to Maria, who dribbles
towards the goal, shoots and scores! Everyone
congratulates Yvette for the assist and Maria for
her first goal of the season. The players head
back to the halfway line for another kickoff.

The goalkeeper dives across the goal to make a great save! The goalkeeper is the only player who may use his arms and hands to catch or block the ball. When he stops the ball from going into the goal, he throws or kicks it back to a teammate. The goalkeeper must have good reflexes and speed — he has a big goal area to guard. In your soccer league you may take turns playing goalkeeper, so it's also good to practise this position.

The referee jumps out of the players' way —
he does a lot of running during a game, too.
The referee watches over the game, making
sure everyone follows the rules and plays the
game fairly. If a player breaks a rule such as
touching the ball with her hands, holding,
pushing or tripping another player, then the
referee blows his whistle to stop the game
and awards the other team a free kick or a
penalty kick.

Teamwork is what soccer is all about. A good soccer team works together to pass the ball, score goals and have fun. Your coach will cheer you on and show you the skills you'll need to be part of the team. Win, lose or tie, all the players cheer for one another and shake hands at the end of the game. Everyone is already looking forward to the next game!

Note to Parents

A child's early sports experiences should be fun. You can help to ensure that these experiences are positive and enjoyable, and will leave your child eager to play again. Find a league that's right for your child. Most neighbourhoods have organized teams for children of all ages and abilities. Look for a relaxed, encouraging environment where the emphasis is on basic skills, fair play, teamwork and fun. Every child should have an equal amount of play time and an opportunity to play each position. And safe practices and appropriate equipment that's in good shape are musts.

Proper supervision is essential. Coaches should know the sport and kids' abilities at different ages. Instruction should be supportive — every accomplishment, no matter how small, should be recognized, particularly in the beginning. Children should be encouraged to compete only against their own past performance.

This way, any improvement will be experienced as success, and children will not compare their performance against others'. Ideally, success should be defined by individual improvement and by having fun, not by winning. After all, this is play, not the pros.

Finally, listen to your child's response to the sport. Your child should make the decision as to whether he or she wants to participate. If the experience does not seem to be positive for your child, try another sport. And remember, continuous reinforcement and encouragement from you are vital to a child just starting out in any sport.

If they enjoy their early experiences, children can grow through sport in many ways. Sport will help them develop their minds and bodies, and gain a sense of accomplishment and self-esteem. Not to mention the fun they'll have and the friends they'll make while playing.